Telephone Tips That SELL!

501 How-to Ideas and Affirmations to Help You Get More Business by Phone

A R T

D1115496

Business By Phone Inc.™
13254 Stevens, Omaha, NE 68137
402-895-9399

Telephone Tips That SELL!
501 How-to Ideas, Tips, and Affirmations to Help You Get More Business By Phone
By Art Sobczak

Published By:
Business By Phone Inc.
13254 Stevens St.
Omaha, NE 68137
(402)895-9399 Fax: (402)896-3353
e-mail: 74051,1402 @compuserve.com

Cover design by George Foster, Foster & Foster, Fairfield, Iowa

Library of Congress Catalog Number 95-083972

ISBN 1-881081-05-2

Contents

About Art Sobczak

Art Sobczak specializes in one area only: working with business-to-business salespeople—both inside and outside—designing and delivering content-rich training programs, seminars, and products packed with ideas, tips, and strategies that users and participants show results from the very next time they get on the phone. Audiences and readers love his "down-to-earth," entertaining style, and low-pressure, easy-to-use, customer-oriented ideas and techniques.

For over 12 years Art has written and published the how-to tips newsletter, *TELEPHONE SELLING REPORT,* subscribed to by over two thousand companies worldwide.

Art is a prolific producer of learning resources on selling by phone. He authored the audio-tape training program, "Ringing Up Sales," published by Dartnell. His video program is "Getting Through to Buyers . . . While the Others are Screened Out." He wrote the book, "How to Sell More, In Less Time, With No Rejection, Using Common Sense Telephone Techniques—Volume 1," and has an entire catalog of other popular training tips tapes and books.

Art's how-to ideas and tips appear regularly in the print and electronic media. He has written a regular column for "Teleprofessional" magazine for 10 years, and is frequently quoted in numerous sales and trade publications and on-line forums.

He holds the popular Telesales Rep College two-day public training seminars nationwide 10 times per year, and also customizes the program for on-site, in-house delivery. Art also delivers how-to programs on effective telesales ranging from one-hour to several days.

Clients include IBM, AT&T, Ameritech, Hewlett Packard,

Norfolk Southern, Baxter Healthcare, and other companies and associations in virtually all business-to-business industries.

His speaking and training reputation has been built as someone who knows what works and what doesn't in telesales because he's done it (corporate telesales positions with AT&T Long Lines and American Express), and still does it. He also conducts extensive research to customize his programs, listening to tapes of actual sales calls of client reps in order to learn the language of the industry, company, and strengths and weaknesses of sales reps and strategies.

Introduction

Dear Fellow Sales Pro,

Welcome, and congratulations on investing in your sales success!

In my over 13 years of training, speaking, coaching on, writing about, researching, and doing telephone sales, I've found one aspect about it undeniable: people love their training information in meaty, brief nuggets . . . morsels they can easily fit into hectic schedules, and digest and adapt. Stuff they can use right now, and get results with.

This handy little book gives you 501 of these gems.

You could breeze through this book and read all 501 tips and affirmations in one sitting. But that would be like trying to rush through everything at Disneyland in a couple of hours—you don't get to truly appreciate the experience. Obviously you bought this book and you can do whatever you want with it, but here's a proven method for getting the most out of these ideas.

1. OK, I'll know you'll do this anyway (I would): *skim* through the entire book. Some of the ideas will

instantly grab you by the collar and shout out, "DO ME!" Start with just one.

2. Reflect on the idea. Apply it to your own situation. That's the way we build habits, through application. Visualize the specific scenario in which you would use the idea or tip.

3. Write it down. If it's a word-for-word tactic, put it into your own words. Then say it out loud (when no one else is around, of course—people will talk).

4. Use it. Just like the Nordic Tracks and Health Riders collecting dust in your friends' basements, none of this stuff means diddly unless you put it into practice.

5. Go through the book again, repeating the process.

Hear These Ideas, and See Them on Your Computer Screen

It's proven that we retain material most when it's delivered in a variety of ways, bombarding our senses from all directions. That's why I suggest you also obtain these ideas in the two other forms I've prepared for you: Get the audio version. Two cassette tapes with yours truly presenting all 501 tips and affirmations. It's a great way to pass the time while on the freeway, while working out, on your way to a sales call, or whenever you want a dose of sales inspiration.

And for those of us spending much of our day hunched in front of a computer screen, imagine looking at your call notes, tugging at your hair in frustration wondering how to get this account to crack. Then, magically appearing on your screen is a tip that gives you a word-for-word idea that is just what you're looking for! Don't laugh. I have this on my computer, and even though I've written virtually every one of these ideas, it's uncanny how you really are forced to think about them when they hit you from your monitor. To order either or both of these tools, call my office at 800-326-7721, or (402)895-9399, or use the order form in the back of this book.

And Finally . . .

If you like what you see here, be like the thousands of others we help every year. I invite you to get and stay in contact with me. Call, write, or fax your success stories. And please do take advantage of the many other telesales resources I provide. Regardless of whether you use the phone for all of your sales, or just to qualify or stay in touch between personal visits, I have resources that can help you do it better, and more profitably. Again, call my office and ask for a free catalog, a seminar schedule, and a sample copy of my TELEPHONE SELLING REPORT newsletter.

Here's to your continued success!

Art

Art Sobczak

Chapter 1

Telephone Prospecting

Always start at the highest level 1
at which you feel your decision
could be made (or even one higher).
It's better to be referred down, since
you can mention the name of the
higher-up who sent you.

When the screener coolly informs 2
you that the person you're asking
for on a prospecting call is no longer
with the company, without missing
a beat, ask, "Who took his/her
place?"

3   **Prior to your prospecting call** to a decision maker, consider talking to actual users of your product/ service within the organization. This will provide great information you can use to prepare your questions.

4   **Selling is nothing more** than helping people buy.

5   **Consider starting at the end** of a directory you're working from when prospecting. Those people have likely received fewer calls from salespeople who typically start at the beginning.

If you have customers you don't 6
bother calling because they're small,
think again. Are they really small,
or are you *thinking* small? Are they
buying things from your competitors they could get from you?
Develop those accounts.

To help understand what moti- 7
vates your prospects/customers, ask
yourself, "What does making their
mortgage payment rely on?" In
other words, what are their most
fundamental needs and concerns?

Have you ever said "no" when 8
you really meant "maybe"? Prospects are the same way. Be persis-
tent in your prospecting.

9 **You reap what you sow.** Be certain you're regularly prospecting to keep your sales pipeline producing.

10 **Whenever your** prospect/customer divulges personal information about family, hobbies, interests, etc., write that information down. It can help build rapport when you bring up the topic on subsequent contacts.

11 **A more positive name** for prospects: unsold customers. Better yet: future customers.

12 **"You rarely, if ever,** hear a person at the top of an organization say, 'It's not in the budget.' So where are you selling?" *David Peoples*

When searching for prospects, 13
don't overlook your existing customers' companies. They can refer you
to different people, divisions, departments, or subsidiaries who
could buy what you sell.

Only have a prospect paged on a
cold call after you ask, "Is that the 14
way he/she typically takes calls?"
Otherwise, you might be interrupt-
ing an important activity, which
could potentially annoy the prospect.

People don't care how good YOU
think your products or services are; 15
they want to know how THEY will
be affected.

16   **If the operator or screener**
      answers the phone, "ABC Company,
      can you hold?", and you know the
      name of your prospect or customer,
      respond with, "Holding for Joe
      Smith, please." You'll avoid the hold
      time.

17   **Always ask for the NAME** of the
      person who makes the decisions
      regarding what you sell, as opposed
      to saying, "I'd like to speak with the
      person who . . ." This way, you
      won't be blindly connected, plus you
      can ask more questions of this per-
      son.

When gathering information on a prospect company, try the sales department. After all, these people like to talk, and can give you tremendously useful info on the company and its direction.

18

Talking to a decision maker without first learning anything about her or her situation is like saying, "I didn't feel this was important enough for me to do any research for."

19

Prospecting opening idea: "We specialize in *(fill in with RESULTS of what you do).* To determine if this would be something you'd like more information on, I'd like to learn a little about your situation. Please tell me . . ."

20

21   **What business are you** really in? If you answer with the *types* of products or services you sell, you're wrong. You're in the business of delivering the results customers enjoy from owning and using your products/services.

22   **For each of your** main competitors, determine where you have advantages. Then develop questions to help prospects actually tell you the competitors' weaknesses: "How long does it take for an outside sales rep to get back to you when you leave a message?"

Do you know why your customers 23
REALLY buy from you? Find out.
Ask your best customers, "We appreciate your business and want to
provide you with what you expect.
What is it you like best about doing
business with us?"

If you don't succeed totally today 24
on a prospecting call, qualify them
for the future: "Pat, if situations
changed, could you see yourself
taking advantage of this offer?" If
so, ask, "What would have to
change?"

Go back to high-potential pros- 25
pects you didn't sell on the first try.
Situations change. Plus, you're a
better salesperson today!

26   **When things are going well**, and you're feeling quite smug with your production, that's the best time to prospect. To keep sales growing, you always need new business to replace what you'll eventually lose. Commit to a consistent number of prospecting calls per day, regardless of how great you're doing.

27   **When prospecting,** and seeking a buyer with a difficult name, ask the operator or screener, "Yes, I'm looking for Dave . . . please help me with the last name here, it's S-M-A-. . . ." They'll say the name for you.

Chapter 2

Working With Screeners

Ask for help from screeners, or anyone at the prospect's organization. It makes them feel special, and will help you get valuable information you'll need to help them buy.

28

Any time there are multiple decision makers involved in the buying process, get the names of all of their assistants as well.

29

30   **If you reach** an answering service, ask when the decision maker typically keeps office hours. Or ask for alternative phone numbers, such as his/her cellular phone.

31   **Ask the screener** to help you get a message to the buyer.

32   **Identify yourself** with your title, if it sounds impressive. "This is Jo Smith, National Account Manager, with Notable Services."

Treat everyone you come in contact with by phone as the most important person in the organization. They just might be.

33

When talking to screeners on a follow-up call, in response to "What is this in reference to?", respond with, "Ms. Bigg and I have agreed to speak again today . . .", if you indeed have.

34

Identify yourself fully . . . first and last name, and company when asking for the decision maker. This answers several of the questions screeners typically ask anyway.

35

36   **After getting the screener's or** executive assistant's name, be sure to note it in your files. Use the name the next time you call. It's a great way to build rapport.

37   **With very inquisitive** screeners, get their help. "You know, I bet you could help me. You probably work closely with Ms. Bigg, right? You probably know the answers to quite a few of these questions."

38   **Screeners are often** your first sale. If their job in the organization is to weed out time-wasting, self-interested salespeople, you need to explicitly communicate why you have something of value worthy of the boss' time.

Talk to the screeners and execu- 39
tive assistants at your own company.
Ask what salespeople say that is
sure to get them screened out. Also,
ask what works in getting to the
decision makers at your company.

Call that tough-to-reach decision 40
maker during his/her lunch, or
before regular starting time. You
might have a better chance of getting through.

Compliment screeners, when it's 41
warranted. *Always* be sincere. It
makes that person feel important, it
builds rapport, and they'll remember you the next time you call.

42 **Build rapport** with the screener so that she/he will work with you and deliver your message personally.

43 **All screeners apply this**—sometimes unspoken—test to callers: "Does this person have anything of interest or value for the boss?" You must be prepared with a results-oriented answer.

44 **Consider mailing** information to the screener before your call. This will help you get to more buyers.

The screener's job is to protect the decision maker's time. Help screeners do their job by explaining the value you have to offer, and you'll get through more often.

45

When you leave a message, ask the screener when the boss will receive it.

46

After building rapport with the screener, gather personal information about the boss. What he or she has hanging in the office, personal momentos, interests . . . valuable information which can help you begin a relationship.

47

48   **Ask for the decision** maker's direct number.

49   **Ask the screener** the times of day you will typically have the best chance of reaching the boss.

50   **Ask the screener** who the boss reports to. This can help you learn the decision-making hierarchy.

51   **Never consider saying** or doing anything that could be construed as deceptive, such as saying it's a personal call when it's not, or saying you're following up on a previous contact when you haven't spoken before.

The buyer's perception of you 52
rises in direct proportion to how
much you know about him and his
situation. Use the screener to collect
that valuable info.

You're not trying to go above, 53
around, through, over, or past
screeners. That mentality is sure to
get you screened out. You want to
work with them so you're perceived
as a professional.

Think about what screeners say 54
about you after they put you on
hold. Are they saying, "It's some
salesperson, want me to dump
him?", or, "There's someone here
who sounds like he has something
interesting."

Chapter 3

Using Voice Mail Effectively

55 **If your main purpose** for a call is one-way communication of information, such as letting a customer know when an order will be delivered, consider making the calls after hours, and leave the messages on voice mail.

56 **Call your own voice mail** when you're away from the office to remind yourself of great ideas you came up with, or important "to get done" items.

Hit "0" or "#" when you reach an electronic switchboard on a prospecting call. This normally routes you to a live person who can provide information.

57

When leaving a voice mail message, speak more slowly than you would in person. This gives the listener the opportunity to take notes.

58

On voice mail messages to prospects or customers you're following up with, give them an action item they can perform between now and the next call: " . . . and if you could have those performance figures ready when I call back . . ."

59

60   **Having trouble getting** through the electronic switchboard? Dial a numeral or two off the main number, and you might be connected to someone's direct line. If the number is 555-1000, you might try, 555-1002.

61   **Prepare your** "voice mail strategy" before your call, just like you prepare your opening and questions. By knowing what you'll say when you reach voice mail, you're able to sound confident and competent.

62   **Every time you leave** a voice mail message, be certain you insert something of interest or value. This ensures they'll return your call, or look forward to your return call.

Chapter 4

Managing Telephone Time

Limit your personal calls while
at work. You'll sell more. Just three
calls daily, averaging only four minutes each comes to 48 hours per
year. How much more could you
earn with another 48 hours of sales
or prospecting time?

63

What percentage of the prospects
in your follow-up file right now will
ever do business with you? The ones
who won't are costing you money
when you continue calling them.
Move them forward or move them
out.

64

65   **After preparing your** "to get done" list for the day, find one item that isn't directly contributing to your success, and get rid of it.

66   **Review your** "To-get-done" list at the end of the day, evaluate anything you didn't accomplish, analyze if it's really worth doing anyway, and if so, put it at the top of tomorrow's list.

67   **Don't be too concerned** about "best times to call." Some reps avoid two hours around lunch, late afternoons, mornings, etc., rationalizing prospects won't be available. If you're not on the phone, you have NO chance of reaching *anyone!*

Have call objectives for the day. 68
When you know you need to place a
certain number of calls, you are
more focused.

If getting started calling each 69
day is the hardest task for you, set
an iron-clad time you will start
every day, no matter what. Make a
commitment to get it done.

The next time you're considering 70
writing a note or letter to communicate a brief point or to request information, call instead. It's amazing
how much time we waste when a
simple phone call gets results instantly.

71   **If a colleague bothers you with idle chit-chat,** stand up. This sends a message that you're busy.

72   **Take each call as far** as it possibly can travel. Don't have a preconceived limiting notion that it takes "x" number of calls to make a sale. If you're on a roll, go with it!

73   **A "No" today is better** than one six calls, or six weeks from now. Get a decision; you can deal with those. Ask the fence-sitters: "What's the probability of us doing business within the next month?"

Plan tomorrow before leaving 74
tonight. Or, on the way home, or in
the shower or on the way to work
tomorrow. Do this every day, and
make the most of your first hour's
worth of calling.

Batch your paperwork or other 75
activities such as sending out brochures or faxes. Set aside time for
these activities so you can call non-
stop for set periods of time.

Commit to making just one more 76
call each day. Try to beat each day's
results. You'll be amazed how much
you can accomplish when you set
your mind to it.

77   **Call every name** on your prospecting list. Jumping around, or prejudging based on some arbitrary excuse wastes time, and might cause you to miss that big sale.

78   **Don't prepare for a call** thinking about one single product or service. Think about determining what the prospect/customer might need, and about offering solutions.

79   **Don't let co-workers steal** your selling time by hanging around when you want to sell. It's like they are taking money out of your wallet, and you wouldn't allow that.

Calculate how much you earn per   80
call. Take average weekly earnings
and divide by average number of
calls per week. Hang that amount of
money on your wall (a $5 bill) for
example, and then try to increase
that average per call every month.

Chapter 5

Grabbing Their Attention and Interest With Your Opening

81 **Your opening statement must** always answer this question for the prospect/customer: "What's in it for me?"

82 **Begin follow-up calls with** proactive phrases like "I'm calling to review/discuss/analyze/go over/ . . ." It's much better than, "Just wanted to see if you had any questions."

When preparing opening state- 83
ments, write as you speak. Use
contractions, informal language,
build in pauses, and use sentence
fragments. Then read it into a tape
recorder and listen to be sure it
sounds conversational.

All opening statements should 84
be scripted. But never read.

On follow-up calls, use phrases 85
like, "I'm calling to continue our
conversation . . .," or, "I'd like to
pick up where we left off . . .".

86   **On calls to inactive accounts,** don't say anything similar to, "You have an account with us, but no activity," Instead, try, "We had the opportunity to work with you in the past, providing you with . . ." Then mention a benefit you can deliver.

87   **After writing out your opening** statement, set it aside for a while. Then come back and be merciless in your editing. Repeat the process until you have one that "sings."

88   **Don't ask for a decision** in the opening statement, such as, "Calling today to set up a time for an appointment." They aren't ready yet. Open with a benefit, moving them into a receptive mindset.

Your customers are someone   89
else's prospects. Be sure that you
have something of value every time
you call. Never take them for
granted, or they might just listen to
the overtures of your competition.

If you insist on using "How are   90
you today?" at the beginning of
calls, please, PLEASE be sure you
sound sincere, and that you listen
and react to their answer.

For every word and idea in your   91
opening statement, ask yourself, "Is
this adding to what I'm trying to
accomplish?" If it's not, edit it out.

92   **If someone answers** the phone and sounds rushed, don't let that scare you into rushing your opening or questioning. Some people naturally sound fast-paced . . . others do it with salespeople until the rep builds rapport.

93   **On a follow-up call**, don't ask if they received your material—assume it. You don't want to make your literature the basis for this call.

94   **Be certain you deliver** your opening in a calm, confident, crisp and articulate fashion. Rushing and mumbling creates an undesirable impression.

Consider mentioning the benefit/ 95
value you can deliver even before
giving your company name. "Mr.
Sims, my company specializes in
helping retailers increase their off-
season traffic. I'm with Precision
Promotions."

You could hardly go wrong by 96
using "Thank you," "Congratulations," or "I was thinking of you,"
as part of your opening, and reason
for calling.

If you feel you must ask for 97
someone's time at the beginning of
a call, ONLY do it after mentioning
the value you can offer, and then
say, " . . . and if I've caught you at a
good time, I'd like to . . ."

98   **Call with new "ideas."** People can resist and object to products and services, but ideas are interesting and create curiosity.

99   **In your prospecting opening**, mention how you've worked with other companies in the prospect's industry, " . . . helping them to . . ." Fill in with the results you've delivered in the past, and could also provide for them.

100   **Whenever you find ways** that other customers use your product or service that could be of value to others, be sure to write that down and use it as a Value-Added Point on future calls. And, get permission to use their name.

To create interest with your 101
opening, mention how you help
solve an industry-wide problem.
"Ms. Prospect, our company specializes in helping convenience stores
minimize employee theft, while not
harming morale . . ."

Opening statement idea to use 102
with regular accounts: "I was re-
cently thinking about you when . . ."
Then fill in the blank with the situation appropriate to them. Everyone
likes to be thought of.

Your opening statement should 103
have two objectives: 1. To move
them to the questioning, and, 2. Put
them in a positive, receptive frame
of mind.

Your opening statement is like   104
the foundation of a building. If it's
weak, the remainder will crumble.

Edit your opening statement by   105
asking, "Is there anything here
someone could potentially object
to?"

You might have the greatest prod-   106
uct or service ever, but without a
compelling opening that grabs interest, you'll never get a chance to
tell your story. Place tremendous
emphasis on creating a superb one.

Chapter 6

Selling With Questions

The quality of the answers you receive is in direct relation to the quality of your questions.

107

The only way to ensure you're making the best presentation possible is to question first. Get information, and then give it.

108

People believe more of what they say than of what you say. Create questions that help them understand and voice their problems and needs.

109

110   **You'll sell much more by** asking questions than by making statements.

111   **Use "playback," or** "parrot" questions to get more information. Simply repeat, as a question, the key part of what the speaker just told you: "You're having delivery problems?"

112   **Question "fuzzy phrases"** for clarification. If they say, "We'll give it some consideration, let's stay in touch," ask what specifically they will consider, when you should speak again, and why that's a better time.

Ask them how they "feel" about 113
an issue. That might give you more
information than asking what they
"think" about it.

The word "Oh?" can be one of 114
your most powerful questions.

Probing technique after hearing 115
a vague comment: "Which means . . .
what, exactly?"

Be specific when looking for 116
information. Don't use words like "a
lot," "often," and "much." As in,
"Does that happen a lot?" Instead
say, "How many times per day does
that happen?"

117   **You can use statements** to probe. For example, "Steve, your thoughts on what you'd like to see in a landscape plan will help me provide the best information."

118   **"I keep six honest** serving men. Then taught me all I knew. Their names are What, Why, and When, and How, and Where and Who."
Rudyard Kipling

119   **Ask "assumptive-problem"** questions that help you learn the details of their problems and needs. "Dale, about how often would you say your supervisors call in sick, when you feel they're really not?"

Another example of clarifying 120
fuzzy phrases. For example, what
does, "We'll give it some consideration," really mean? Ask them,
"That's good to hear. What, specifically will you be considering?"

Resist the tendency to jump into 121
a presentation after uncovering just
a sliver of a need. Continue questioning to further develop and embellish the need or problem.

If you get a question you'd pre- 122
fer to defer until later, turn it
around explaining why. "In order for
me to quote you the very best price
for the system that would meet your
specific requirements, I'd like to
learn a little more about . . ."

123 **Before going into your** presentation, to ensure you haven't missed anything, ask them, "Jan, before I make my recommendation, is there anything else I should know about your situation?"

124 **Use "loaded problem/benefit"** questions. "Many of our customers found they were having problems getting their orders filled within seven days with the other service. What is your experience?"

125 **When talking to a prospect** who called you in response to your advertising, ask them, "What was it that caught your eye in the ad and prompted the phone call?" This can help you immediately zero in on their hot button.

Before sending out information, 126
ask, "Let's assume that you like
what you see when you get it. What
happens next?"

Use opposite choices when ques- 127
tioning to understand their desires.
"Are you looking for deluxe office
space in an office tower complex, or
something more along the lines of
an industrial park location?"

Avoid using the hanging "or . . ." 128
when questioning, as in, "Is this
something you'd use, or . . .?" It's
confusing to the listener, and shows
a lack of confidence. Just ask the
question, then be silent.

129   **Don't qualify your** questions with wimpy words like, "I don't want to seem pushy, but . . .," or, "You might not want to answer this, but, . . ."

130   **Embellish the needs** you uncover by layering more questions on their responses. For example, "And then what happened?" "What implications does that have on the other departments?" "How does that affect the bottom line?"

131   **Any time you send** out a sample or demo, always first ask, "What criteria will you use to evaluate it?"

Try the "Triad" question: "Most of   132
our customers use us because of our
X, Y, or Z. (fill in with your benefits/
results). Which of those are of most
interest to you?" *Bill Bishop*

With indecisive prospects you   133
obviously have shown you can help,
ask, "Pat, you're waiting for . . .
what . . . . before we can work together?"

Avoid asking "What are your   134
needs?" This expects them to do your
job. Instead, pick out a specific need
you can fill, and question about it:
"What are you experiencing with
downtime?"

135   **Question to learn the** decision-making process: "What is the normal procedure at your company for making a decision like this?"

136   **Any time you hear your** prospect or customer mention someone else in the company with regards to what you're offering, ask them, "Oh, what do they do?" This helps you learn of all the players involved, and the process.

137   **Customers buy based on** value. But not what you *think* is value. It's what their perception of the value is. Ensure you know what they're looking for, then deliver it.

Help them imagine ownership, by   138
saying, "Let's say you already
owned this. How would you . . .?"

Whenever sending out a pro-   139
posal, or when you're competing
against other vendors for the business, ask, "What are the top three
considerations you'll use to make
your final decision?"

A tactful way to go over their   140
head after you learn there are other,
higher decision makers involved:
"Would it help you at all if I called
her directly?" Or, "Would it save you
some time if I contacted her?"

141   **Layer questions,** one on top of another after their responses, to learn their real emotions.

142   **Use instructional questions,** such as, "Please tell me . . .," "Share with me . . .," "Give me some idea of . . .," and "Please explain how . . .".

143   **On your next follow-up** calls, ask yourself, "What, specifically, is this person interested in? Why am I calling him back?" Unless you can answer with a precise, detailed explanation of the value they're looking for, you need more information.

Present at least two alternative 144
answers when probing for sensitive
information: "Would you say your
budget this year is closer to $50,000
or $100,000?"

Explain your reason first when 145
asking for sensitive information:
"I'm asking this next question,
because it will help me make the
best recommendation for your situation. What were your total sales of
that product last year?"

Avoid the use of "Really" as a 146
question in response to their statements. It's meaningless, and annoying.

147   **Ask prospects what** criteria they used the last time they selected a supplier. Then ask if they learned anything useful from that process.

148   **Never go into a pitch on** an incoming call when the inquirer asks you for information. Instead, respond with, "I'll be happy to help you. So I can provide the best information for your situation, please tell me about . . ."

149   **Get clarification, always.** Their definition might be different than yours. For example, "When you say 'fast turnaround,' what is your definition of that?"

Money Question: "How have you typically financed a purchase like this in the past?"

150

Money Question: "What type of budget do you have set aside for this?"

151

Money Question: "What amount did you have in mind for this type of program?"

152

Money Question with an Evasive Prospect: "What budget figure are you thinking of for this project? Ballpark figure."

153

154 **Find out if there are other** players involved by asking, "If you decided to pursue this, who else would be sitting in on the final decision?"

155 **Another way to learn** of other influencers in the decision-making process is to ask, "Who will you consult with when you're evaluating your decision?"

156 **People will go to greater** lengths to avoid pain than they will to seek pleasure. Think about the pain you help people avoid, and ask questions to get them thinking about that potential pain.

Ask the number of questions at 157
one time that they'll answer at one
time: one. Don't pile on questions;
they'll get confused and answer the
easiest one.

Probe for dissatisfaction. Ask 158
them what they're receiving now
from their present vendor, and then
ask them to compare that to what
they expected, or would ideally like
to have.

After you feel you have the sale 159
cinched, but it won't take place for a
few weeks, ask them, "To prepare
for the unforeseen, could you see
anything happening that would
possibly hold this up?"

160   **Be curious.** Build a desire to visualize everything that's going on in your prospect's environment.

161   **Don't ask if you may** ask them a question. That's a question itself, for gosh sakes! Just ask the question.

162   **A salesperson said,** "I can lead them to water, but I can't make them drink." The wise, seasoned manager responded, "You don't want to MAKE them do anything. You just want to help them realize they're thirsty!"

A benefit is only a benefit if the   163
person hearing it perceives it to be a
benefit . . . at that very instant.
Ensure you're presenting benefits
by questioning first.

To find out what your prospect is   164
paying now with a competitor, ask,
"What are the costs for . . .?" This
usually works better than, "What is
ABC Company charging you?"

If you detect the prospect is just   165
looking for multiple bids, ask them,
"If our proposal is the best, will we
get the business?" Then ask, "How
will you judge the best?"

166   **Good salespeople ask** questions. *Great* salespeople know how they'll respond when they hear the answers . . . especially the answers they'd rather not hear.

167   **Ask questions to help** them quantify their needs. Use "How much?", "How often?", and, "What does that cost you?" to get them to understand their problem in tangible terms.

168   **If they must speak** with someone else before making a decision, ask them, "Are you personally sold on doing this?" If they're not, don't let them off the phone until they are sold, or you know why not.

Chapter 7

Listening for Sales

Pause after you ask a question. Resist the tendency to answer for them, or to keep talking.   169

Take notes. It helps you to not interrupt, and to recall key points of your phone conversation.   170

If someone misunderstands your statement or question and begins answering something you really didn't ask, resist the tendency to interrupt. Remember, as long as they're talking, you might learn some valuable information.   171

172   **Words don't mean; PEOPLE**
mean. Listen for the tones and
feelings behind the words.

173   **Visualize the person** speaking to
you at the other end of the line.
This helps you listen, as well as put
enthusiasm in your voice.

174   **Don't be flustered when** someone answers your call in an appar-
ent rush. Many people do this naturally. Gauge their responses to your
opening and initial questions. If
they are running out the door, offer
to call back at a better time.

To increase your attention span 175
on calls, after the prospect makes a
statement react by asking yourself,
"How can I use this information to
help this person buy?"

Pause after *they* answer a ques- 176
tion or make a statement. This
ensures you don't interrupt, and
allows them to give you more information which will help you help
them buy.

Clear your desktop of distrac- 177
tions while on calls. Never read
newspapers, memos, or anything
else while they are talking. Give
them 100% attention.

178   **Listen 80% of the time** on the phone, and talk 20%. What they have to say is much more important than what you have.

179   **Putting yourself in the** prospect's position will help you to listen more effectively.

180   **Listen for the feelings** behind the words. They might not always say what they really mean.

181   **Practice listening on the phone** and off. Make a point to listen more carefully to everyone you come in contact with when you leave to-night.

If you're presenting and hear 182
someone else talking to your prospect in his background, simply stop
talking yourself. Obviously he isn't
hearing you. Then wait until he
comes back.

When talking, pretend you're 183
holding a burning match. If you
don't get feedback from them before
the match reaches your fingers,
you'll get burned!

NEVER interrupt. It's rude, and 184
deprives you of valuable information.

186   **Listen for activity** in the prospect's background. If you detect he's right in the middle of something and distracted, offer to call back at a more convenient time.

187   **LISTEN!** (enough said).
A wise old communicator

188   **When you hear an emotional** word or idea that gives you the itch to interrupt, write the word down instead. Wait until they finish, then ask them to go back to the previous idea.

Silence doesn't mean they're 189
resisting you. In face-to-face set-
tings, people are often silent as they
ponder their buying options.

Their desire to listen to you goes 190
down in direct proportion to the
amount of time YOU speak.

Force yourself to be silent more 191
often in all of your face-to-face
conversations today, and notice how
much more you'll learn.

Be paranoid about talking too 192
much. Every time you speak for
more than 30 seconds, set off a
mental alarm to remind yourself to
get some feedback.

193   **Encourage your prospects** to continue speaking with "reflective" listening phrases such as, "Go on," "Tell me more," "And then what happened," and, "Please continue."

Chapter 8

Persuasive Presentations

Before presenting your benefits, 194
after your questioning, bridge with
something like, "Don, based upon
what you told me, I believe we have
the system that is ideal for what
you're looking for."

Instead of presenting all of your 195
"benefits," present only a few, but
in several different ways. After
identifying their interests, use vari-
ous terms to describe the feelings
they'll have by buying from you.

196   **Use the words "for instance,"** and, "for example" when stating what your product/service can do. This reminds you to personalize and tailor the benefit to their specific situation.

197   **Customers buy for** their reasons, not yours.

198   **Get your prospects** and customers physically involved to bridge the communications gap: "Karen, take a look at page five of the proposal and I'll show you what . . ."

199   **Drop their name** in at the beginning of a sentence to grab their attention.

Avoid statements that are easily
challenged, such as, "We're the most
respected in the business." Instead,
back up claims with proof, or third-
party references, "Our customers
consistently give us 99.9% satisfac-
tion ratings."

200

At the end of a presentation,
ask them, "What haven't I covered
yet that's important to you?"

201

Number your benefit points for
impact. "Gail, there are three main
results you'll get from this program.
First . . ."

202

203   **If you've determined you can** help them in some way, every day that goes by without them buying means they have missed out. Point this out if they stall.

204   **When you're in a** competitive situation with several other suppliers to win the business, ask to be the last to present. You can ask about the other presentations to learn valuable information.

205   **Once you've determined** their interests, mention the most appropriate benefits several times. Psychologists say that messages become more firmly embedded when they're repeated.

When you speak from personal 206
experience about your product/ser-
vice, be sure they know that. For
example, "I have one myself, and
what I like is . . ."

When you're faced with silence, 207
resist the tendency to just continue
talking. Instead, get them to open
up. Ask, "How do you feel about that
last point?"

State your price with convic- 208
tion. Sometimes a salesperson's
tone when stating price says, "This
is a starting point on price, and it's
very negotiable."

209   **Guarantees are necessary** for credibility, but don't sell your guarantee harder than you sell your value. Some reps use the negative sell just to get a "yes," and then later get exactly what they sold: people asking for their money back.

210   **Mention the competition's** price in terms of dollars, while presenting yours with numbers. "Their price is two-hundred and fifteen dollars. Ours is only one-ninety-eight."

211   **Never assume** that your prospect or customer knows what your product or service can do for him. Once you know his needs, state your benefits and results specifically.

If you have nothing to gain,   212
monetarily, from them buying from
you, point that out. Many prospects
and customers are skeptical of sales
reps who are on commission.

Point out the disadvantages of   213
what you have, if there are any.
You'll be viewed as more credible,
with nothing to hide.

Forget about benefits. Think in   214
terms of the "results" you deliver.

Paraphrase their needs by say-   215
ing, "Based on what you told me,
what you're looking for is . . ."

216   **Help them associate** the savings they can realize with you to something they'll easily understand. "The savings you'll show with this system every month could make the payments on one of your delivery vans."

217   **If they, or you, can say** "So what?" to what you think are benefits, don't use them. The points are not strong enough.

218   **Preface your benefits with** positive statements that paint an exciting mood: "And here's one of the aspects that our customers tell us they really like best about our service . . ."

Just SAYING you have experi- 219
ence means little. Instead, be specific with examples. "I have a list of
20 satisfied customers in your industry who say they would do the
same thing again."

If you've uncovered a problem 220
you can solve, one that is costing
them money, point out how much
they are losing every day.

When presenting huge volumes 221
and prices, be certain to project with
unwavering confidence. Sometimes
reps give the feeling, through their
voice, that they are ashamed or
afraid of presenting such a large
number.

222   **Use action to describe** your product/service. People can visualize motion better than abstract ideas.

223   **If there's a concern** or objection that inevitably comes up, address it before they do. Say, "And if you're asking yourself about _____" Then proceed to present the benefits of why that's not really an issue.

224   **Get feedback after presenting** your value points. "How would that work for you?" "Does this sound good so far?"

225   **"If we can differentiate** a dead chicken, you can differentiate anything." *Frank Perdue*

Use the word "investment" 226
instead of "cost" or "price," and
"invest" instead of "spend."

It's never good to knock the com- 227
petition, but it's OK to let the customer do it. Ask questions in areas
where you know you're superior, or
where the other vendor has problems: "What do you do when you
have after-hours service needs?"

Brainstorm for emotional, de- 228
scriptive, and visual terms to help
your prospects see and feel the
results you deliver. Use familiar
comparisons. For example, "It's
very lightweight . . . about the same
as your standard desktop office
stapler."

229 **Ask them to retrieve your** catalog or sample so they can go through it with you by phone. This bridges the visual gap, and gets them physically and visually involved.

230 **Repeat their jargon,** language, or pet words to make your points. If they said "Get the ball rolling," several times, you could strategically drop it into your presentation to add impact. This helps you to connect more powerfully.

231 **When presenting** your price, always attach a value statement to it. "Of course you'll get free delivery, one month's worth of supplies, and installation, all for only $795."

Help them imagine already owning and using your product or service. "Let's just assume for a mo-
ment that you did have this unit in
your office. What are the functions
you'd use it for?" This helps reduce
resistance.

232

If you've identified specific prospect needs and problems, but yet
they're reluctant to commit to a
sale, ask them, "What would happen if you do nothing?" This helps
them understand the problem isn't
going away on its own.

233

Emotional words that sell include, "guarantee," "easy," "worry
free," "saves," and, "helps you . . ."

234

235 **Use third party** references to build credibility. "Our customers say . . .", "People who are now on the system find that . . .", "Current users tell us that . . ."

236 **Use stories in your presentation.** It helps them see themselves enjoying the benefits you deliver. Especially so when you put them in the story.

Chapter 9

Using a Sales Language

Never begin an answer to a question with the word "no." It taints everything you say afterwards. Instead, say what you can do . . . the possibilities.

237

Don't use five words when one will do. For example, use "now" instead of, "at this point in time." Use "because" instead of "due to the fact that." Use "many" instead of "a great number of." Think of the wordy phrases you use.

238

239   **Use the words** "you" and "your" to help them visualize themselves already enjoying the results of what you have to offer.

240   **Saying "Do you understand?"** or "Are you following me?" is insulting. Instead, place the burden on yourself: "Did I explain that clearly enough?"

241   **Be specific about times** and dates. Don't say, "I'll call you sometime next week." Instead, ask, "Would next Thursday at 1:30 be a convenient time for you to speak with me again?"

While in your car (preferably 242
alone!) pick out a billboard, a building, or an object, and practice de-
scribing it in colorful, emotional,
desirable terms. Use plenty of inflec-
tion. Avoid words like "thing" and
"stuff."

Use "self-disclosure" to build 243
rapport. That means sharing of
yourself as well as asking questions.
For example, "I know what you
mean. I do the same thing," or, "I've
been in that situation too."

End calls with a positive, instead 244
of the self-demeaning, "I don't want
to take any more of your valuable
time." Simply say, "Thank you. I
look forward to our next conversation."

245 **When dealing with** an irate customer, don't refer to their issue as a complaint. Use terms like, "situation," "concern," "this matter," or "misunderstanding."

246 **Avoid using the word** "just" to belittle yourself and your importance. For example, "I was just calling today . . ."

247 **Avoid saying,** "I was going through my records here and decided to give you a call . . ." That is impersonal, and doesn't make them feel special.

Don't ask, "What don't you like about your vendor?" That could attack their decision-making ability. Instead, ask, "What would you like to receive that you might not be getting now?" 248

Avoid words that put them on the spot, such as "Of course you will agree . . .," "Everyone knows that . . .," "And of course you'd want that, wouldn't you?" 249

Annoying words and phrases to avoid: " . . . things like that," "uhhh," "I mean . . .," "you know." 250

251   **The impressions you make** in your first two seconds of communication are so vivid, it takes another four minutes to add 50% more impression—positive or negative—to that communication. *Bert Decker*

252   **To direct them back** to business after going off on a small-talk tangent, transition by saying, "Getting back to what we had discussed earlier . . .," then ask a question.

253   **People love to be right.** When you hear something you agree with, respond with, "I agree," "That's right!", "Great point," and "Very perceptive."

Avoid saying "I'll be honest with 254
you . . ." It's a waste of words. Plus,
people might wonder what you were
when you didn't say it.

Avoid internal company jargon or 255
acronyms. It confuses the listener.

Avoid the negative, "salesey" 256
phrases, "I'm sure you'll agree . . .",
and, "Of course you know . . ." It's
annoying, and usually causes resistance.

Avoid the use of "disclaimers" like 257
"I might be wrong, but . . .," and, "I
could be mistaken, but . . ." People
want definite answers, not wishy-
washiness.

258   **Use "when" instead of** "if" to help your prospect visualize himself enjoying your benefits. For example, "When you use this system, you'll find yourself breezing through your projects in a fraction of the time it took before."

Chapter 10

Getting Commitment (Closing)

Ideally, if you've done everything   259
right, they will sometimes volunteer
the sale. But don't count on it.
Simply and directly say, "Let's
finalize the details, OK?"

Don't always judge success by
the "yes" answers you get. Measure   260
your attempts. Set a goal for the
number of times you'll ask for the
business today. Celebrate when you
reach that goal. The sales naturally
follow.

261   **If they like what you** have, and say they'll buy the next time they have the need, do everything you can today to ensure that sale. Open the credit-approved account, get a preapproved blanket purchase order from them . . . whatever, to make the purchase easier.

262   **Closing Question:** "Gene, we seem to be in agreement that this is what you're looking for. What do you suggest we do?"

263   **Instead of jumping** on the first buying signal you hear, question it to help them strengthen their convictions. If they said, "This really would work for us," ask them, "In what areas would you show the most benefit?"

Closing Question: "Kelly, what can we do together to speed up the process and make this happen?"

264

You'll lose 100% of the sales you don't ask for.

265

Ask for commitment with conviction.

266

Closing Question: "Are you thinking about getting three of them?" Use whatever amount would be just a tad higher than what they likely would do. This prompts a decision, or more conversation.

267

268   **Those who expect more,** get more. Don't sell yourself short when asking for the sale. Ask big.

269   **A question to help** them determine what should happen next: "What is the next step?"

270   **Closing Question:** "We could have this delivered and operational by Tuesday. What would you like me to do?"

271   **Help them visualize** themselves owning and using your product/service. "If you had this, how do you feel you'd utilize it?"

To upsell, don't mention the next   272
price break, as in "You can get a
better deal if you buy 50." Instead,
simply mention how many more
they need to get the price. "You'll
save $1.50 per unit by getting only
five more."

Trial Closing Question: "Amy, do   273
you think you would be happy with
this type of service?"

Maintain a positive, confident,   274
steady tone of voice and rate of
speech when asking for the sale or
commitment. Some reps clutch up
and lose it at this point.

275   **State the agreement** you've
reached, then ask for the major
commitment: "Jan, since we're in
agreement that this is what you're
looking for, and it's within your
budget, let's go ahead and get the
paperwork started, OK?"

276   **Closing question:** "Sounds to me
like you've already decided to go
with this. Am I right?"

277   **Closing question:** "Do you have
further questions, or are we ready
to proceed?"

278   **Closing question:** "Any reason to
wait any longer?"

Closing question: "Is there any- 279
thing else you need to know to move
ahead with this order?"

Closing question: "Are you ready 280
to start going over the final details?"

Listen for "possession signals," 281
signs that they've already visualized
themselves using your product/
service. "What we'd likely do is train
a couple of people at each location."

The main reason customers don't 282
buy more from their vendors: they
aren't asked to by the vendor. Be
sure you're satisfying every need
you possibly can.

283   **When you're writing** up an order, don't say, "Anything else?" We're all conditioned to say "No." Instead, make a tangible recommendation based on what they're already getting, then ask for the sale.

284   **Buying signals** can indicate the time to begin closing. But, consider asking another question or two. This can help them further strengthen their reasons for agreeing with you.

285   **"Pushiness" only occurs** when you try to sell something they don't want or need. Asking for the sale is not being pushy, assuming you've questioned effectively and made the appropriate recommendation.

Don't just wish for the sale: "I just wanted to let you know these do come in several colors, and we could even custom order one for you." Be sure there is no question that you are ASKING for it.

286

Leave no doubt you want their business.

287

Tie the timing of the next call into their commitment to take action. "What day do you feel we should speak, so you'll have enough time to collect those figures?"

288

What's the worst that could happen if you ask for the sale? How about the best? The worst never happens.

289

290   **A Trial Closing Question:** "Quite a deal, isn't it?"

291   **It's easy to increase** order sizes by adding complementary items or services. Simply say, "Many people who get ____ also find ____ to be of great value because (fill in with the results they realize)." It costs nothing to try this technique!

292   **Take their temperature** all throughout the call. "How do you feel this would work?" "What do you think about . . .?" "How does this look compared to . . .?" Their agreement is your sign to continue. Any resistance is dealt with early.

Closing Question: "Why don't we   293
give it a try?"

Ask "as if" assumptive questions,   294
such as, "Where would you use this
if you had it?" "Who would use it?"
"How would it work for you?" This
helps them visualize themselves
already enjoying the results.

When not having much luck   295
with prospects who are happy with
their present vendor, ask for a trial
order as a last resort: "Would you
like to try us just on a smaller trial
basis? This way you can sample our
service and delivery without com-
mitting all of your business."

296   **Closing question after** buying signals have been heard: "Will two dozen (pick your own figure) be enough?"

297   **Get commitment by** positioning yourself as the expert. Use powerful phrases like, "I recommend," "I suggest," "I invite you to . . ."

298   **Ask for decisions.** Don't let people put you off. It wastes your time and money. Equate getting a decision—yes or no—with success.

299   **Closing Question to** Begin Wrapping Up the Details: "I'm ready to talk terms if you are!"

Trial closing question: "So I've answered all of your questions?" 300

Closing Question: "Can you think of any reason why we shouldn't go ahead with this?" 301

Temperature Checking Question: "Are you ready to move forward with an order, or do you have further questions?" 302

Closing Question As a Last Resort When All Else Fails: "Well, would you use us as a secondary vendor for things that are not available with your present vendor?" 303

Chapter 11

Building a Powerful Selling Voice

304   **Your body positioning** affects the way you sound. Right now, assume the position you would take if you were calling your biggest potential customer ever. Use that position for all of your calls.

305   **Be certain your tone** of voice and enthusiasm are at as high a level all day as they were at the beginning of the day.

Your attitude is conveyed about 20-30 times more powerfully over the phone than it is in person. Be certain your voice projects your positive attitude.

306

You're not calling names, leads, reply-card inquirers, or directory listings. You're calling PEOPLE, with real needs, concerns, and desires.

307

Open your mouth wider when speaking by phone. This helps you enunciate more clearly.

308

Loud voices are annoying. Deepen your voice instead to make a point.

309

310   **Articulation exercise:** Read this several times- "If, I, Place, an, invisible, comma, after, each, word, and, an, invisible, semicolon; after, some, words, my, speech, has, presence." This forces you to enunciate.

311   **Practice your tone** and articulation by reading children's books aloud.

312   **Regardless of how many** calls you placed or received today, your next one is the first one to that person. Treat it like the only one for the day.

When you greet someone on an   313
incoming call, view it as escorting a
friend into your home. You wouldn't
be frowning or acting indifferently.
Greet them warmly, with enthusiasm.

Practice tongue twisters to   314
articulate clearly. Recite this one
now, several times while picking up
speed each time: "Frank phoned
four pharmaceutical factories feeling fresh and fulfilled."

Place a couple of warm-up non-   315
sales calls at the beginning of the
day to get your voice and mouth in
gear.

316   **Eliminate "fillers"** like "uh" and "ah" from your speaking. It detracts from your message, and makes you sound less intelligent.

317   **Perform an** "articulation warm-up" before starting your calling for the day, in order to get your speaking mechanism in gear. Try repeating, "The tip of the teeth, the lips, and the gums."

318   **Many people speak** in more of a monotone than they realize. Practice consciously taking words and ideas and punching them with more emphasis. It feels awkward initially (like all new habits) but becomes second nature.

Chapter 12

Addressing Resistance and Objections

Upon hearing an objection, 319
respond with the non-adversarial
statement, "Let's talk about that."
Then proceed with questions to get
them talking about their reasons
for objecting.

If things were flowing smoothly 320
on the first call, but, suddenly on
the second call they are a totally
different person, simply ask, "Pat,
the last time we spoke I had the
impression you loved this idea.
What happened since then?"

321   **If you hear price** resistance, ask them, "Is it more of a money-availability question, or a value question?"

322   **Buyers usually aren't** looking for the lowest-priced vendor. They typically want the least-risk vendor. Determine how you can position yourself as the least-risk supplier.

323   **If you hear the obvious** brush off, "I don't think we need that," at the beginning of a call, respond with, "I'm not yet sure if you do, either. That's why I'd like to ask a few questions to determine . . ."

There are no price objections, 324
only value questions.

Before writing off a prospect who 325
you're obviously getting nowhere
with, ask, "Would you say we'll
likely never do business together?"
This might prompt them to say
never is a long time, which gives you
a lead-in to more questions.

Take each of your top five com- 326
petitors and determine your main
advantages over them. Then develop
questions to get prospects talking
about their needs in those areas. For
example, "How are you now affected
by the order fill rate you're getting?"

327   **When they want** to "Think it over," ask them, "In what areas are you still not convinced?"

328   **When you hear** an objection, to hear the reason behind it, respond with, "I'm not sure I understand." They'll likely respond with more detailed information.

329   **After addressing** resistance, and there's silence, ask for commitment or the sale again. Don't make it easy for them to delay or serve up another objection.

330   **To get them talking** after they state an objection, say, "Tell me more about that."

The objection you hear consists   331
only of the words which represent
the symptom of the real problem.
That's what you must address to be
successful. Do it with questions.

The old myth says that "The sell-   332
ing doesn't start until an objection
has been expressed." That's gar-
bage. If the sales process had been
perfectly executed, an objection
wouldn't even occur.

Resistance early in a call is   333
easier to deal with than a major
objection later on. Plus it helps you
change course when necessary. So,
ask for the resistance if it's there.
"What are your thoughts so far?"

334   **If there's a common** objection
everyone you contact usually brings
up, mention it before they do, along
with the answer. "And you might be
wondering if . . ."

335   **Get to the heart** of the reason for
an objection: "It seems the real
decision here is this: is (the ulti-
mate benefit they'll receive) more
important than (the objection)?"

336   **Never tell someone** they're
wrong (even if they are!). Instead,
take the responsibility. "I don't
think I explained myself clearly.
Here is what I meant . . ."

To help the indecisive prospect move: "What would happen if you did nothing?" 337

If they put you off with, "Call back in six months," verify they are sincere. "OK, so what you're saying is that you are interested in doing business together. It's just that now is not a good time?" Then find out what will happen in six months making that a better time. 338

Use the "Just suppose" technique. "Just suppose the money was in the budget. Would you go with it then?" 339

340   **Question to ask** when they are comparing you to a discounter: "What other expenses have you considered in the long-term if you went with the lower-price alternative?"

341   **Don't focus all** your energy thinking of answers for objections. First start with the many reasons someone might have for stating an objection. Work on understanding them, and then on questions to help them talk about those reasons.

342   **Another question to ask** when they compare you to a discounter: "How long do you plan on keeping the unit?" This helps you amortize the difference over a longer period.

Create urgency by pointing out   343
what they're missing every day they
delay. "Pat, we've agreed that by
using our system you'd generate
about another $100 daily in walk in
traffic, sales you're missing every
day now."

Don't mail information just to   344
get it out the door, especially with
people who have no short-term
potential. Instead, let them qualify
themselves. "Would it be worth it to
send you information for your files,
just in case things change with
you?"

345   **If on a follow-up call** they immediately say they haven't read your
literature yet, reply, "That's OK. As
long as I have you on the phone, let
cover a few points . . ." Take advantage of the opportunity.

346   **If a prospect says that** your price
savings wouldn't be large enough to
switch, ask him, "How much would
you have to increase sales to generate the same NET profit as the
savings we'd provide over a year?"

347   **Your literature doesn't do** the
selling for you. If it did, your company wouldn't need you.

Instead of blurting out "Why?", 348
which can sound argumentative,
ask, "Oh, what has lead to that
decision?"

In response to a "Send literature" 349
brush-off, try, "I'll be happy to. Let's
say you like what you see. What will
happen next?" Or, "Will you be
ready to buy at that point?"

Initial resistance at the beginning 350
of a prospecting call is quite natural.
It's a reflex instinct. Quite often
prospects will say, "I'm happy with
what we have," as an attempt to get
off the phone. Be prepared with a
question to get them talking.

351   **Objections are only** symptoms of a larger problem. Unless you identify the problem, you'll never address the true concern.

352   **You'll never change** anyone's mind by trying to overcome an objection with a slick phrase. The best you can do is get them to doubt their beliefs. You do this by questioning.

353   **An alternative to asking** "Why?" is, "Apparently you have a reason for feeling that way. May I ask what it is?" Then respond with, "If you weren't concerned with that, do you feel we could move forward?"

When you hear a price objection, 354
try asking, "If price were not an
issue for you, would this be the
system you'd choose?"

If you ever have to give conces- 355
sions, do it grudgingly. Giving in too
quickly diminishes the value of it,
and might cause them to keep grind-
ing away.

Respond to the stall, "I want to 356
think about it," with, "That usually
means you have a money-related
question, or a question I haven't yet
answered. Is that right?"
Bill Bishop

357   **If budget is the problem,** ask them, "What have you done in other situations where there was something you wanted that could help your department, but it wasn't budgeted? How did you get it?"

358   **To learn the reason** behind their objection, ask, "Oh? What led to that conclusion?"

359   **If someone claims** to be getting a better deal or offer elsewhere, question every component of it to determine if you're comparing "apples-to-apples." You can determine if they're mistaken, if they're putting you off, or if the deal is better.

If they tell you to call back "in a few months or so," respond with, "I'll be happy to. What will make that a better time for you?"   360

Upon hearing an objection, instead of mentally arguing with it, ask yourself, "Under what circumstances could that be true?" This helps you understand why they say what they do.   361

When a prospect tells you they're happy with who they're buying from, ask them, "When you do have to replace your products, or return them, what are the main reasons?" This gets them thinking about problems . . . things you can solve.   362

363 **Paraphrase objections** and resistance as questions to ensure you understand the situation, and to position them as something to be answered—not overcome. For example: "What you're asking is, if you'll get a return on the extra $200 you'd pay with our system, is that the question?"

364 **Questions and objections** should never leave you at a loss for words. Every time you hear a new one, brainstorm three or four ways you'll respond next time. Write them down in a notebook, and study them until they're committed to memory.

People love to buy, but they hate to be "sold," with "sold" meaning being pitched a product or service they have no need or use for. Help them buy!

365

When your prospect is fence-sitting after repeated calls, ask them, "Pat, on a scale of 1-10, with 10 being the most interested, where would you say you are right now regarding our offer."

366

If you hear, "I want to shop around," ask them, "What will you be looking for?" This might help clear up any misunderstandings about what you could provide, and cause them to forgo the shopping and buy from you now.

367

368   **Learn the real reason** for the resistance. You only waste time chasing shadows. Ask, "If I understand what you're saying, this is the only factor holding you back, is that right?"

369   **Repeating their objection** as a question can get them to explain it more fully. "You don't feel you could use us this year?" And if it's not a real objection, it can prompt the real answer.

370   **Instead of caving in on price** with someone who wants to negotiate, be prepared with low- or no-cost "giveaways" with perceived value that you can offer instead. Get creative.

If you're reaching a dead end, 371
ask them, "Under what circumstances would you see yourself
using a service like ours?"

Chapter 13

Wrapping Up the Call

372   **When preparing** to wrap up a call, ask them, "Ok, what is going to happen next?" This prompts them to detail what they will do as a result of this call.

373   **Summarize at the end** of every call. Review, 1. What they will do next; 2. What you will do next; 3. What will happen on your next conversation.

374   **Offer to mail materials** to the other people your prospect will speak with in making the final decision.

To help qualify a prospect's com-   375
mitment, and to solidify it, ask
them to send YOU something after
a call. For example, a brochure,
product sample, invoice from a
present supplier. It gets them more
involved, and gives you useful information.

Ensure they know what will   376
happen on the next call. Don't say,
"I'll just touch base with you . . ."
Tell them, " . . . and on our next
contact we'll review the results of
your meeting, and talk about details
of a proposal."

377   **After the call** ask yourself, "What did I like?", and, "What would I have done differently?" You'll reinforce the positives, and learn from the negatives so they don't occur again.

378   **Put ideas for opening** statements in the notes from this call. What a great time to think about what you'll say on the next call!

Chapter 14

Other Ideas You Can Use

Use USA Today's "Across the
USA" section to pick up on news in
your prospect's/customer's area. You
can use this information to build
rapport, and they'll be impressed.

379

Whenever a satisfied customer
raves about your company, products,
or services, write down the com-
ments, or have a "Testimonial" file
in your word processing program.
Or, ask them to send you a letter.
Use these on calls.

380

381   **Call the Telesales Tips Line** to hear a newly recorded sales idea each week: (402)896-TIPS. That's (402)896-8477.

382   **Penetrate deeper into** the customer's company. Get their assistance. "Pat, who else in your organization would be able to take advantage of the same benefits you're getting?" Ask them to make the introduction.

383   **When asking for referrals**, help them brainstorm, "Who else do you know . . . maybe people in your trade association, perhaps some of your other suppliers, how about other divisions of your company?"

Send a note or post card today to a customer you haven't spoken with in a while. It keeps your name in front of them. You never know when they might have a need for what you sell before your next scheduled call to them. 384

Send a novelty or promotional item to make your package stand out. You can mention it when you call back. "Mine was the package with the pepper shaker that said 'We can spice up your sales'." 385

Whenever you pick up an incoming call, always greet the person with enthusiasm, as if they were the most important person in the world. They'll feel like it! 386

387 **When you find a news clipping** that your prospects/customers would have interest in, copy it and mail it to everyone it would be appropriate for. Include a brief note. This further positions you as someone who delivers value.

388 **Shop the competition.** Call them. See how they handle calls. Get their literature.

389 **Ask good customers** to provide you with information and literature on competitors who call them.

390 **Tape record your calls** and exchange tapes with a co-worker. Provide each other with feedback.

If you want your letter to stand 391
out, avoid mailing it Friday.
Monday's mail is typically the
biggest pile. Take it home, and mail
it Saturday morning. Tuesday is
usually the slowest mail day.

If it sounds as if they're using a 392
speakerphone (and you're not talking with a group), say, "I think we
have a bad connection here. I can
barely hear you." They'll typically
apologize, and pick up the handset.

When they answer their phone 393
with their first name, that's im-
plied permission to use it also. As
in, "Hi, this is Karen." Using Ms.
or Mr. here would put up a barrier
of formality that doesn't exist.

394   **Have them take out** their calculator to run the numbers with you. It bridges the visual gap, and gets them physically involved.

395   **Never put off calling** a customer who you think is going to complain. Their problem won't go away on its own. And by solving it, you can strengthen their loyalty. Plus, they likely just want someone to listen to them.

396   **With your letters,** write like you speak. No one ever says, "As per our conversation," "Please advise," "Enclosed please find . . ." So don't write that way either.

Set appointments for your next 397
follow-up telephone call. Be specific
with the date and time. This shows
you're a professional, and that you
mean business. Plus it helps you
manage your calls efficiently.

Get referrals by asking: "Who 398
else do you know who also has a
similar problem and would like to
get the results you've experienced?"
Help them: "Someone in a trade
group? Perhaps someone in another
city?"

Don't just tell a prospect or cus- 399
tomer you'll try to do something for
them. Tell them you'll DO it, and
then follow through.

400   **Write on the outside** of large envelopes of literature. For example, "Pat, here's the catalog we discussed by phone." This helps your material stand out, plus reminds them of what you spoke of.

401   **Upon calling back** a prospect who seemed interested on the first call, but cooled down considerably, find out why: "Mr. Prospect, we seemed to agree that this would solve a few problems. What has happened since our last call?"

402   **When your prospect/customer** needs to confer with someone (or says they will), ask them, "Are you going to recommend that this is what you do?" This ensures they are sold first.

A tension relaxer: Drop your head to your chest, roll it to the right, nearly touching your shoulder. Roll it back and to the left. Return to the upright position and repeat the process slowly as you feel yourself relaxing.

403

If you're placing a follow-up call, assign "homework" so that they're doing something between now and the next contact. This way you know they are committed.

404

Understand the organizational hierarchy of the purchasing decision for your product/service. Through what departments must it travel, who must sign off on it, and what paperwork must be completed?

405

406   **Write down every promise** you make to a customer or prospect regarding what you'll do or send. Then check your list every day. Unfulfilled expectations fatally damage relationships.

407   **Sincere compliments** always have, and always will be an effective way to build rapport and good feelings. Use words like "Congratulations," "That's quite an accomplishment," "You should be proud," and "I admire you for that."

408   **When you or your company** wrongs a customer, listen, let them vent, then ask them what should be done. It's likely what they request will be less than you're able to give.

When your customer changes
companies, offer to call him at the
new one to continue the relationship. And be sure to quickly contact
his replacement to build a new
relationship with that person. But
don't assume you'll keep the business. Work for it.

409

If you call nationwide, keep a
road atlas at hand so you can pull it
out at appropriate times to visualize
where the prospect is.

410

Don't make the mistake of taking for granted that your customers
will automatically think of you
when a need arises. Stay in regular
contact to build "mind share,"
working to keep you and your
company's name in mind.

411

412   **Regardless of whether** you sell a product or intangible service, everyone sells the same thing: the end RESULT of using or owning that product or service.

413   **Instead of saying** "How are you today?" at the beginning of a call, TELL them how they are: "You sure sound great today!"

414   **Be sure you** use a P.S. in your sales follow-up letters. The P.S. is often the first part of the letter that is read. Make it benefit-packed.

Write notes on the back of your business cards and clip them to your literature. They just might keep the card!

415

View yourself as a consultant to your customers' businesses. You are helping them maximize their success and the success of their business.

416

"Focus on what customers want and need, help them buy what's best for them, and make them feel good about it." *Michael LeBoeuf*

417

Be sensitive of how you react to unusual names. Usually the best reaction is none at all.

418

419   **Dropping price can cost** your company money in more ways than one. Everyone, regardless of the price they pay, expects the same level of service.

420   **The way you accept** compliments says a lot about you and the way you are perceived. Don't be apologetic: "Oh, it's nothing really." Or, "I got lucky." Instead, use a simple "Thank you," or add, "we worked hard on that project."

421   **Drink warm water** when you're on the phone. Cold liquids, especially colas, tend to constrict the vocal cords, and cause build-up in the mouth.

Be sure to take detailed notes
after the call. Confucius said, "Poor
handwriting better than poor
memory. "

422

For mailing follow-up literature,
have bright stickers made up with,
"Here's the Information We Discussed By Phone." This helps your
material move to the top of the pile.

423

Always tell people where they
are being transferred, and the direct dial number of that person,
just in case the call is dropped.
Better yet, stay on the line to intro-
duce the other person.

424

425   **When a committee** is involved, ask your prospect if it would help if you were to address the committee on a conference call.

426   **If they ask about your price,** that is evidence they could get value from your product/service. Your job is to raise that value higher than the price.

427   **If you ever give a price** concession in a negotiation, get something in return. Ask for a larger quantity, a longer contract, or something that suggests you don't drop prices on a whim.

Look around your desk area. Do you have enough prompts hanging up, information you can access on calls to help you sell? Take advantage of the fact they can't see you, and surround yourself with sales aids.

428

Write out difficult names phonetically. This avoids embarrassing mispronunciations.

429

Take each call as far as you possibly can. Don't assume that you couldn't make a sale on a first or second call.

430

431   **Make a point to call** one inactive customer per day. Mention the fact you've done business before, question to uncover needs similar to the ones that lead them to buy from you before, and then offer something of value. Calling 250 inactive customers in a year will likely get you FIVE TIMES more business than the same number of cold prospecting calls.

Chapter 15

Self Motivation Tips and Affirmations

When you hear a "no," it's not
YOU, personally, that's being re-
sisted . . . it's an idea that's objected
to. Analyze your "no's" and learn
from them.

432

Play to win, instead of to not lose.
Too many sales reps take the safe,
warm, cozy path . . . avoiding any
potential resistance—and missing
sales in the process. Go for the
gusto!

433

434 **Don't judge your success** solely by your sales. Celebrate the number of attempts. The more you ask, ultimately the more you'll receive.

435 **Have a secondary objective** for every call, defined as, "At minimum, what do I want to accomplish with this person?" Make it something you'll likely be able to achieve. This ensures you'll never experience rejection.

436 **Prepare for each call** by asking, "How can I help this person?"

You'll never rise above the level   437
of your own self-perception. Define
and visualize yourself as the top
professional you are capable of
being. Believe in that vision, and
commit to becoming that person.
And keep reaching higher!

Those who can proudly count
their only failures on one hand   438
aren't so eager to list their only
successes on the other.

Your imagined, self-imposed limits   439
are always closer than any real ones.

440   **End today, and every day,** with a positive call. Whether it be a sale, or a secondary objective that you achieved, it helps you leave with an upbeat attitude, and lets you start with one tomorrow.

441   **Practice doesn't make perfect.** PERFECT practice makes perfect. If you keep doing the same things over and over that don't result in the success you want, you become more skilled at achieving undesirable results.

442   **"Behold the turtle.** He makes progress only when he sticks his neck out." *James B. Conant*

Over the course of the calling 443
day, set mini-goals for yourself . . .
checkpoints along the road. For
example you could segment your
day into thirds or quarters, with a
goal for a number of calls at the
end of each segment.

"The more I learn, the more I 444
realize how little I really know."
Einstein

You haven't made your best 445
sales call yet. Strive to make it the
next one.

It doesn't matter if someone else 446
says you can't do it. It only matters
if YOU say it.

447   **Preparation is required** for successful calls. But don't suffer from "planning paralysis." Remember, you need to be on the phone to succeed.

448   **"If you are going to** be thinking anyway, you may as well think big. Most people think small because they are afraid of success, afraid of making decisions, and afraid of winning. And that gives people like me a big advantage." *Donald Trump*

449   **How many people** have you made smile today? Do it at least one more time.

Reward yourself after a big sale you've worked hard to get. A nice dinner, new clothes, a trip, maybe even a house or car!

450

Think back, right now, to several of the sales or accomplishments you are proudest of. Seize that feeling. Recall what you were doing, think-ing, and how you were interacting with others in order to accomplish those things. Repeat them!

451

Ask yourself assumptive ques-tions. "What's the best way for me to increase my sales by 15% this month?" Then, answer in terms of possibilities.

452

453   **No customer or prospect,** manager or supervisor, can stress you out. You can only ALLOW others to get to you.

454   **"If you think you can** or you can't, you're always right."
Henry Ford

455   **Nothing of monumental** significance has ever been achieved without it first having been set as a goal. **What great things** are you going after right now?

Laugh often, especially at silly 456
mistakes (as long as you learn from
them). Too many people take themselves way too seriously, and their
performance and health suffers as a
result.

"If what you did yesterday seems 457
big, you haven't done anything
today. And when you're through
improving, you're through."
Lou Holtz

Your rewards are in direct pro- 458
portion to what you wager. Dare to
go after the big accounts, and put in
the time to do what's necessary.
Your return will be commensurate.

459   **After 5,000 attempts** to come up with the carbon impregnated filament, someone asked Thomas Edison why he was wasting time on failures. He responded, "I've not failed. I've successfully identified 5,000 ways that do not work."

460   **Sales superstars consistently** do what the average sales reps don't or won't do.

461   **Put forth effort as if** every day is the end-of-quota period, and you need to meet that goal.

462   **Knowledge isn't power;** the *application* of that knowledge is power.

Success comes before work only 463
in the dictionary.

You can't steal second base with 464
your foot still on first. In order to
succeed, you need to stretch yourself and take a risk.

There are very few things that 465
you can gain from by saying "no" to,
other than illegal, immoral, and
physically harmful activities. Don't
shy away from opportunities.

"One of these days . . ." often 466
results in "If I only would have . . ."

467   **Big expectations tend** to show big results. Think, and act large.

468   **Rejection is not an experience.** It's how some people *define* an experience. You'll never be rejected again if you can pinpoint something positive that comes from every call.

469   **Be more like a kid** on the phone. Kids: 1. are not bothered by no's; 2. take risks; 3. are imaginative; 4. have high ambitions; 5. have great attitudes; 6. are constantly active, and, 7. are curious.

The all-time leading base stealer
in baseball history, Rickey
Henderson, is also the all-time
leader in another category: Caught
Stealing. No one dwells on that, nor
should you dwell on the "no's" you
encounter in your pursuit of successes.

470

Just DO it! And do it now!

471

Here's a way to beat call reluctance: Ask yourself what is the
worst thing that could happen on
the next call? Perhaps get screamed
at and insulted personally? It's not
going to happen, so place that next
call!

472

473   **Don't settle for** "good enough."
That's defined as just enough to get
by and survive. Always put in that
little extra.

474   **Why is it that** the hardest working
people seem to have all the luck?

475   **In order for someone to** become
a "natural" at any skill or profession, they need to be "unnatural"
first. That means putting in the
practice and effort to reach that
level. In order to golf in the 70's,
you must go through the 80's first.

"The world behaves differently 476
when you actually take action to go
after what you want. What you
wish 'could be' starts becoming.
The dream moves in your direction,
begins to come to you, even as you
reach for it." *Price Pritchett*

Zig Ziglar says, "What you do off 477
the job determines how well you'll
do on the job." Invest in yourself.

You are among an elite group of 478
salespeople. Simply by using your
words, ideas, and voice, you are able
to persuade people to take action by
phone. Not everyone can do that.
You are special!

479 **So what if you heard** a "no" on your last call? And who cares if you hear another one today, which you likely will if you continue calling. As long as you learned from the experience, and did your best, you can feel proud.

480 **What would you try** or do if you knew you could not fail? Get a picture in your mind. Then go for it! If you haven't done it yet, it's simply a false limitation.

481 **Don't be affected** by the "naysayers." Someone will always try to bring you down, complaining about the quality of leads, lack of support, or anything, for that matter. Times are tough only for those who THINK so.

What would you need to do to 482
increase your sales by 50%? Brainstorm a list of 10-20 possibilities.
Notice that you're thinking in terms
of what you could do, not what you
couldn't. Pick out a few of those
ideas and work on them!

Place another call immediately 483
after a success or a sale. Keep the
momentum going when you're "in
the zone"!

On your very next call, make a 484
point to SMILE. You'll feel better,
and so will they.

485   **Keep in mind that the large** prospect you're waiting to call is buying from someone, but will eventually change. It might as well be from you!

486   **To beat call reluctance,** think of all the successes you've had when you dug in your heels and took action. Nothing but guilt and regret results from wasting time, avoiding the phone. Pick it up now, and equate action with accomplishment!

487   **Set short-term activity** goals, such as number of prospecting calls in a two-hour period. It keeps you focused, active, and invigorated.

End every call on a positive 488
note, regardless of the outcome. You
enhance your image, you feel good,
they feel good, and you leave the
door open for future contacts.

Prepare yourself emotionally
before each call. Ask yourself, "Am I 489
ready to talk to what might be my
most important customer ever?"

If you must doubt anything, 490
doubt your limitations.

491   **There are no "born"** salespeople, any more than there are natural pilots or brain surgeons. Expertise comes through desire, work, and practice. To appear to be a "natural" means you must put in the work first.

492   **The "no" you received** on the previous call has nothing to do with the results you'll get on your next call . . . unless you let it affect you negatively. Get back at it, and place that next call!

493   **Every call you place** or receive should provide information which will make you a better salesperson. Learn something from each experience.

"The only risks that aren't a little   494
scary are the ones you've out-
grown."   *Price Pritchett*

ACTION cures fear; ACTION   495
vaporizes stress; ACTION builds
confidence; ACTION beats call reluctance; ACTION gets results.

Regardless of the name of the   496
organization writing your paycheck,
view yourself as being self-employed.
More than any other profession, you
control your destiny, just as entre-
preneurs. It's your own business, so
make it a success!

497   **Commit to making just** one more call each day. Try to beat each day's results. You'll be amazed how much you can accomplish when you set your mind to it.

498   **Place your most dreaded** calls at the beginning of the day. You realize that they weren't so bad, you start the momentum earlier, and you get more done.

499   **Remind yourself** that you are an important person. You have something of value that will make the lives better of the people you call.

Preparation breeds confidence. 500
The more prepared you are before a
call, the more self-assured you feel.

The worst time to think of what 501
you'll say next is right before you
say it. Be prepared with your open-
ings, questions, and responses to
resistance and questions.

Overdeliver on your promises. 502

Read this book again, and again, 503
and again. Each time you'll find new
nuggets you'll use.

Here Are Other Resources You Can Get Right Now to Help You Close More Sales Using the Phone!

Have Information In Seconds With Business By Phone's Fax-Back Service

Within seconds you can have detailed descriptions of resources that can help you get more business, and help make your job easier. Go to the handset of your fax machine, call (402)896-9877, listen for the prompts, press "1,"and follow the instructions. When asked, press "101" as the document you'd like. This is our Fax Information Directory listing all of the brochures and samples available to you by return fax. Receive this document, pick the additional information you'd like, then call again to receive your choices. Or, simply use the document numbers on the next page to make your selections.

FREE Training! Call the Telesales Tips Line

Each week hear Art Sobczak of Business By Phone present a new recorded sales, motivation, or communication tip you can use right now. Call,

(402)896-TIPS

Get a FREE Subscription to Business By Phone's Catalog of Tapes, Books, Telesales Rep College Seminars, Other Training Materials

If you use the phone in any aspect of sales or service, you'll find something in this catalog to help you do it better. Also, especially if you didn't buy this book through us, you'll want to be listed in our database so you can be one of the first to be notified of the newest available resources for telesales reps and managers. Call our offices at 1-800-326-7721.

"Telephone Tips That SELL!
*501 How-to Ideas, Tips, and Affirmations to Help
You Get More Business By Phone"* By Art Sobczak
Computer Screen Saver Version: Yes, have all of
the tips you've seen and used here in this book appear,
effortlessly, on your computer screen at whatever
intervals you wish. It's like having your own personal
sales coach! Works with Windows and Windows 95.
Order Fax Information Document #501 for a brochure.
$39.95 (+$3.50 shipping).

Audio Cassette Tape Version: Hear Art provide you
with over two hours of all 501 of these tips on two
audio cassettes. Order Fax Information Document #501
for a brochure. **$29.95 (+$3.50 shipping)**.

**"How to Sell More, In Less Time, With No
Rejection, Using Common Sense Telephone
Techniques—Volume 1"** *By Art Sobczak*
A fine complement to the book you're now holding,
and a must-have for successful sales pros. In this 220-
page book, Art Sobczak details **more,** instantly-usable
ideas on all parts of the sales call. If you liked this
book, and are looking for more in-depth treatment to
these ideas, you'll find it here. The title of the book
says it all. Guaranteed! Order Fax Information Document #114 for a brochure. **$29.50 (+$3.50 shipping)**.

To Order Any of These Items
1. **Mail your check,** *(U.S. funds only)* **to Business
By Phone, 13254 Stevens St., Omaha, NE, 68137.**
2. **Call us at 1-800-326-7721.**
3. **Fax your order with credit card number to
(402)896-3353.** *(Overseas shipping billed at cost.
Canadian shipping 2x listed rate.)*

To Get More Copies of This Book, And the Audio Taped and Computer Screen Saver Versions:

To get additional copies of this book, and/or the audio taped or computer screen saver version, photocopy or remove this form, or call or fax us with the necessary information. *(Inquire about quantity discounts. Also, bookstore and dealer inquiries welcome.)*

❑ *Please Send* **Telephone Tips That SELL!**

____ books @ $14.95 (+$3.50 shipping)

____ audio tape sets @ $29.95 (+$3.50 shipping)

____ computer screen savers @ $39.95 (+$3.50)

____ SAVE! All Three for only $69.95 (+$7 shipping)

Name_____

Company_____

Address (Street address only please)_____

City_____**State**_____**Zip Code**_____

Phone_____

Fax_____

Method of Payment

❑ Visa/MC/AMEX/Discover

\# _____

sig._____exp._____

❑ Check /Money Order Enclosed *(U.S. Funds Only)*

Ways to Order

- **Phone** your order to **1-800-326-7721**, or (402)895-9399.
- **Fax** your order to (402)896-3353.
- **Mail** your order to Business By Phone, 13254-B1 Stevens St., Omaha, NE, 68137.
- **E-Mail** your order: 74051.1402 @ Compuserve.com.